Animal Fac

Vicky Shipton

OXFORD
UNIVERSITY PRESS

A hippo

mouth

It has a big mouth.

A lion

teeth

It has big teeth.

A rabbit

ear

It has big ears.

A bushbaby

eye

It has big eyes.

5

An anteater

nose

It has a big nose.

A giraffe

neck

It has a long neck.

An elephant

ear

trunk

It has big ears and a long trunk.